A LITTLE GIANT® BOOK

RIDDLES

Joseph Rosenbloom

Illustrated by Sanford Hoffman

STERLING

New York / London
www.sterlingpublishing.com/kids

Library of Congress Cataloging-in-Publication Data

Rosenbloom, Joseph.
     The Little giant book of riddles/ by Joseph Rosenbloom; illustrated by Sanford
Hoffman.
     p. cm.
     Includes index.
     Summary: A collection of hundreds of illustrated riddles, arranged in such cate-
gories as "Outlaws and Lawpersons," "Science for Dummies," and "Fun Food."
     ISBN 1-8069-6100-7
     1. Riddles, Juvenile. [1. Riddles. 2. Jokes.] I. Hoffman, Sanford, ill. II. Title.
PN6371.5.R6123 1996
818'.5402--dc20

                                                              96-9811
                                                                 CIP
                                                                  AC

LOT#: 10 9 8
08/13

Published by Sterling Publishing Co., Inc.
387 Park Avenue South, New York, NY 10016
Material in this collection was adapted from *Mad Scientist: Riddles, Jokes, Fun;
School's Out: Great Vacation Riddles & Jokes:: Get Well Quick!* (published in paper
as *Super Sick Jokes & Riddles*); *Wacky Insults & Terrible Jokes; Wild West Riddles
& Jokes,* and *World's Best Sports Riddles & Jokes,* all © by Joseph Rosenbloom ©
1996 by Sterling Publishing Co., Inc.
Distributed in Canada by Sterling Publishing
c/o Canadian Manda Group, 165 Dufferin Street
Toronto, Ontario, Canada M6K 3H6
Distributed in the United Kingdom by GMC Distribution Services,
Castle Place, 166 High Street, Lewes, East Sussex, England BN7 1XU
Distributed in Australia by Capricorn Link (Australia) Pty. Ltd.
P.O. Box 704, Windsor, NSW 2756, Australia

Sterling ISBN-13: 978-1-4027-4972-8
          ISBN-10: 1-4027-4972-4

For information about custom editions, special sales, premium and
corporate purchases, please contact Sterling Special Sales
Department at 800-805-5489 or specialsales@sterlingpub.com.

CONTENTS

1. Go Directly to Jail *5*

2. Outlaws and Lawpersons *19*

3. Meanwhile . . . Back at the Ranch *41*

4. Play Ball! *59*

5. Science for Dummies *73*

6. Fun Food *93*

7. Having a Wonderful Time *103*

8. Are We Having Fun Yet? *125*

9. Back to Mother Nature *147*

10. Birds of a Feather *163*

11. Healthy, Wealthy and Weird *169*

12. Get Well Soon! *191*

13. Fighting Words *215*

14. The Not-So-Great Outdoors *229*

15. Far Out! *263*

16. Driving Yourself Crazy *275*

17. Playing Around *295*

18. Go for the Gold *319*

19. Broken Down on the Information Superhighway *329*

20. Moving Right Along *339*

Index *344*

1. GO DIRECTLY TO JAIL

Why did the clock get arrested?
Because it struck twelve.

Why can't you keep a clock in jail?
Because time is always running out.

What hired killer never goes to jail?
An exterminator.

Why did Robin Hood steal from the rich?
Because the poor didn't have any money.

What is the difference between a jeweler and a jailer?

A jeweler sells watches; a jailer watches cells.

How many prisoners can you put into an empty cell?

One. After that the cell isn't empty anymore.

How are prisoners like astronauts?

Both are interested in outer space.

Why do prisoners like to eat a lot of sweets?

They are hoping to break out.

Why did the prisoner take a shower before he broke out of jail?

He wanted to make a clean getaway.

How is a person in jail like a sinking ship?

Both want to be bailed out.

Why are prisoners in jail the slowest talkers in the world?

They can spend 25 years on a single sentence.

How is an escaping prisoner like an airline pilot?

Both want safe flights.

Why was the picture sent to jail?

Because it was framed.

What did the police do in the shoe store?

Rounded up the sneakers and the loafers.

What kind of bars won't keep a prisoner in jail?

Chocolate bars.

What kind of party do prisoners like best?

A going-away party.

Why did the Sheriff arrest the chicken?
It used fowl language.

A prisoner was in jail. All he had in his cell was a piano. Yet, he managed to escape. How did he do it?

He played the piano until he found the right key.

Why were the clothespins arrested?
For holding up a pair of pants.

Why were the tennis players arrested?
Because they had racquets.

Why were the pair of old watches arrested?
Because they were two-timers.

Why were the walls arrested?
Because they were holding up the ceiling.

Why was the stale loaf of bread arrested?
It tried to get fresh.

Why was the deck of cards arrested?
The joker was wild.

Why is it dangerous to play cards in the jungle?
Because of all the cheetahs.

Why did the Sheriff arrest the cook?
For beating the eggs and whipping the cream.

When is a jail not on land and not on water?

When it is on fire.

What did the thief get for stealing the
calendar?
Twelve months.

Why was the photographer arrested?
*He shot his customers and then blew them
up.*

Why was the fisherman arrested?
For packing a rod.

What did the burglar get for robbing the
rubber band factory?
A long stretch.

Why is it hard to keep a bank robbery
secret?
*Because so many people who work in the
bank are tellers.*

What kind of candy would a doomed
prisoner like to have before he is hanged?
  A Life Saver.

What did the comic say when the gangster
stuffed a dirty piece of cloth in his mouth?
"That's an old gag."

What show do prisoners like to put on?
A cell-out (sell-out).

What do you call a sheep that hangs out with forty thieves?
Ali Baa Baa.

What do you call an elephant that hangs out with forty thieves?
Ali Babar.

What do you call someone who steals soap at camp?
A dirty crook.

How do hangmen keep up with current events?
They read the noose-paper.

What is the favorite sport of executioners?
Hang gliding.

What did the hangman give his wife for her birthday?

A choker.

What did the prisoner about to be hanged say when he was pardoned at the last minute?

"No noose is good noose."

2. OUTLAWS & LAWPERSONS

Why were outlaws the strongest men in the Old West?

They could hold up trains.

Why did outlaws sleep on the ground after they robbed a bank?

Because they wanted to lie low.

Who pulled the biggest holdup in history?
Atlas — he held up the whole world.

Which way did the varmint go when he stole the computer?

Data-way.

Who was the most famous cat in the Wild West?

Kit-ty Carson.

Who was the thirstiest outlaw in the West?

The one who drank Canada Dry.

How do you make a strawberry shake?

Introduce it to Jesse James.

Where do dead outlaws go on Saturday night?

To ghost towns.

What happened when the outlaw ran away with the circus?

The Sheriff made him bring it back.

What kind of cat chases outlaws?
   A posse cat.

Who robbed stagecoaches and wore dirty clothes?
   Messy James.

What has red bumps and is the fastest gun in the West?

Rootin' Tootin' Raspberry.

What is small, purple, and dangerous?

A grape with a six-shooter.

What is green and dangerous?

A thundering herd of pickles.

How did the Sheriff find the missing barber?

He combed the town.

Why did the Sheriff go to the barbecue?

He heard it was a place to have a steak out.

Why did the outlaw hold up the bakery?

He kneaded the dough.

What is the hardest thing to deal with in a poker game?

A greasy deck of cards.

Why did the outlaw steal the deck of cards?

He heard there were 13 diamonds in it.

Why didn't the sailors play cards?

Because the captain was standing on the deck.

What does a pickle say when it wants to enter a poker game?

"Dill me in."

Why did the outlaw hold up the river?

He heard it had two banks.

What is the difference between an outlaw and chocolate cake?

One hits the mark; the other hits the spot.

Why did the outlaw wear loud socks?

So his feet wouldn't fall asleep.

What lives in the ocean, has eight legs and
is quick on the draw?

Billy the Squid.

Who is the toughest pickle in Dodge City?
Marshall Dill.

Where do most of the nuts in Dodge City
hang out?
At the Hershey bar.

Who is the meanest goat in the West?
  Billy the Kid.

What did the banana do when it saw Billy
the Kid?
  The banana split.

Why did Billy the Kid set Dodge City on fire?

So he could be the toast of the town.

What was Billy the Kid's favorite subject in school?

Triggernometry.

What kind of bandit steals cats?

A purr-snatcher.

Two outlaws robbed a bank. They decided to bury the money they stole. If it took two outlaws five days to dig a hole, how many days would it take them to dig half a hole?

None. You can't dig half a hole.

Why is a saltine like an outlaw?

Both are safecrackers.

What did the outlaw give his wife for her birthday?

A stole.

30

What is small and yellow and wears a mask?
The Lone Lemon.

What happened when the painter threw his pictures at the outlaw?
The outlaw had an art attack.

When is an outlaw neither left-handed nor right-handed?
When he is underhanded.

What do outlaws eat with their milk?
Crookies.

What kind of sweets do outlaws steal?
Hot chocolate.

What do you get if you cross a big bell and an outlaw?
A gongster.

Why did the gang of outlaws suddenly
leave the restaurant?

Because they had finished eating.

What is the difference between an outlaw and a church bell?

One steals from the people; the other peals from the steeple.

Why couldn't the chuch steeple keep a secret?

Because the bell always tolled.

What would you get if you crossed Jesse James and a cow?

Better not try it. Jesse James doesn't like to be crossed.

What would you call a short, sunburned outlaw riding a horse?

Little Red Riding Hood.

Why wasn't the outlaw buried in the town cemetery?

Because he wasn't dead.

Why did the outlaw hold up air-conditioned banks?

To get cold cash.

When is a pistol like a young horse?
  When it is a Colt.

How is a stolen pistol like a racing car?
  They're both hot rods.

When is a gun unemployed?
  When it is fired.

How come a duck won the shoot-out?
  It was a quack shot.

What would happen if an ice cream cone picked a fight with Jesse James?
  The ice cream cone would get licked.

What do you call Jesse James when he has the flu?
  A sick shooter.

What is a shotgun?
  A worn-out rifle.

What do you call a baby rifle?
  A son-of-a-gun.

What would you get if you crossed a clock and a gun?

A ticks-shooter.

What is the safest way to talk with an outlaw?

By long distance.

Why did the outlaw carry a bottle of glue when he robbed the stagecoach?

So he could stick up the passengers.

Why did the outlaw brush his teeth with gunpowder?

So he could shoot his mouth off.

Why did the cowboy put a whistle in his ten-gallon hat?

So he could blow his top.

Why did the banana run from the outlaw?
  Because it was yellow.

Why did the outlaw shoot the clock?
  He was just killing time.

What happened to the outlaw who fell into the cement mixer?

He became a hardened criminal.

Did you hear about the stupid outlaw? When he saw a sign saying, "MAN WANTED FOR ROBBERY," he applied for the job.

What did the ten-gallon hat say to the outlaw?

"I've got you covered."

3. MEANWHILE...
BACK AT THE RANCH

What cattle follow you wherever you go?
Your calves.

Where do calves eat?
In calf-eterias.

Where do cattle eat?
In re-steer-rants.

What key do cattle sing in?
Beef-flat (B-flat).

What did the bored cow say when she got up in the morning?
"Just an udder day."

What goes out black and comes in white?
A black cow in a snowstorm.

Can you spell COW in thirteen letters?
SEE O DOUBLE YOU.

Why don't most cows go to college?
Because not many graduate from high school.

Why did the cow go to the psychiatrist?
It had a fodder complex.

What do cows give after an earthquake?
Milk shakes.

What is the easiest way to keep milk from turning sour?
Leave it in the cow.

What is a calf after it is a year old?
Two years old.

Why don't cows have money?
Because the farmer milks them dry.

How is a political speech like a steer?
There is a point here and there and a lot of bull in between.

What do you call a cow that has lost its calf?
De-calf-inated.

Why is it better to own a cow than a bull?
Because a cow gives milk, but a bull always charges.

What is the best thing to do if a bull charges you?
Pay him.

What would you have if cattle fought each other?
Steer Wars.

How do cowboys drive steers?
With steer-ing wheels.

How do you make meatloaf?
Send a cow to the seashore.

When was beef at its highest?
When the cow jumped over the moon.

Where do cows go for entertainment?
To the moo-vies.

Where do bulls go to dance?
To the meatball.

Where do cows go to dance?
To a dis-cow-theque.

What music do cows like to dance to?
Cow-lypso (calypso) music.

There were three tomatoes on a shelf. Two were ripe and one was green. Which one is the cowboy?

The green one. The other two are redskins.

Why was the bowlegged cowboy fired?

Because he couldn't get his calves together.

What do you do with a green cowboy?

Wait until he ripens.

What kind of ponchos do Mexican cowboys wear on a rainy day?

Wet ones.

In what kind of home does the buffalo roam?

A very dirty one.

What has six legs and walks with only four?

A horse and rider.

What is the most important use for cowhide?

To keep the cow together.

When is it good manners to spit in a rancher's face?

When his mustache is on fire.

What has four legs and can see just as well from either end?

A horse with its eyes closed.

When is a horse not a horse?

When it turns into a stable.

How long should a horse's legs be?

Long enough to reach the ground.

What always follows a horse?

Its tail.

What kind of horse eats and drinks with its tail?

They all do. No horse takes off its tail to eat or drink.

What is the hardest thing about learning to ride a bucking horse?

The ground.

Why did the cowboy saddle up a
porcupine?

So he wouldn't have to ride it bareback.

How much do you have to know to teach a horse tricks?

More than the horse.

An outlaw went on a trip on Friday, stayed three days, and came back on Friday. How was that possible?

His horse was named Friday.

What kind of horses frighten ranchers?

Nightmares.

Why are horses always poorly dressed?

Because they wear shoes but no socks.

What was the fastest way to ship small horses in the Old West?

By Pony Express.

What smells good and rides a horse?

The Cologne Ranger.

How do you make a horse float?

Take two scoops of ice cream, root beer — and add one horse.

What did the rancher see when he fell off his horse?

An all-star show.

Are horses good acrobats?

Yes, they can turn cartwheels.

What part of a cowboy's outfit is the saddest?

Blue jeans.

If dogs have fleas, what do sheep have?

Fleece.

What did the cowboy say when he wanted to get the sheep's attention?

"Hey, ewe!"

What does a sheep say when it has problems?

"Where there's a wool, there's a way."

What does a male sheep do when he gets angry?

He goes on a ram-page.

Why do sheep go into saloons?

To look for the baa-tender.

Why is a rodeo horse rich?
It has a million bucks.

Which part of a horse is the most
important?
The mane (main) part.

Why is it hard to recognize horses from the back?

Because they are always switching their tails.

What did the horse say when it finished eating a bale of hay?

"That's the last straw!"

4. PLAY BALL!

What position do pigs play on a baseball team?

Short-slop.

What was a spider doing on the baseball team?

Catching flies.

When do monkeys play baseball?
  In Ape-ril.

What kind of hit do you find in the zoo?
  A lion drive.

What has 18 legs and catches flies?
  A baseball team.

What has two gloves and four legs?
  Two baseball players.

How do you hold a bat?
  By the wings.

When is an umpire like a telephone operator?
  When he makes a call.

What kind of umpires do you find at the North Pole?
  Cold ones.

What's the difference between a rain barrel and a bad fielder?
  One catches drops; the other drops catches.

Why did the umpire penalize the chicken?
For using fowl (foul) language.

What is the difference between an umpire and a pickpocket?

The umpire watches steals, the pickpocket steals watches.

How are tough teachers like umpires?

They penalize you for errors.

What does a skunk do when it disagrees with the umpire?

It raises a stink.

Why was night baseball invented?

Because bats like to sleep during the day.

Why did the ball player blink his eyes?

He needed batting practice.

What would you get if you crossed a lobster and a baseball player?

A pinch hitter.

Why was the mummy sent into the game as a pinch hitter?

With a mummy at bat, the game would be all tied up.

What would you get if Mickey Mantle married Betty Crocker?

Better batters.

What do you get if you cover a baseball field with sandpaper?

A diamond in the rough.

Why is a baseball field hot after the game?

Because all the fans have gone home.

Why can't turtles play baseball?

They can't run home.

How can you pitch a winning baseball game without ever throwing a ball?

Throw only strikes.

What happens when you hit a pop fly?

The same thing that happens when you hit a mom fly.

Where in a baseball stadium do the fans wear the whitest clothes?
In the bleachers.

What is the difference between a queen who likes to dance and a baseball player?
One throws balls, the other catches them.

What does an umpire do before he eats?
He brushes off the plate.

Where do coal diggers play baseball?
In the minor (miner) leagues.

Why couldn't Robin play baseball?
He forgot his bat, man.

Why don't baseball players join unions?
Because they don't like to be called out on strikes.

66

Where do great dragon baseball players go?

To the Hall of Flame.

What is the difference between someone who hits the ball but does not score — and someone who beats a chicken?

One fouls the hit, the other hits the fowl.

Why was the chef hired to coach the baseball team?

Because he knew how to handle a batter.

Which takes longer to run: from first base to second or from second base to third?

From second base to third, because there's a shortstop in the middle.

Why did the silly baseball fan take his car to the game?

He heard it was a long drive to center field.

Why couldn't the fans get soda pop at the double-header?

Because the home team lost the opener.

Why did the outlaw gang try to steal the baseball field?

Because it was the biggest diamond in the world.

Which baseball league has the most trees and shrubs?

The bush leagues.

Why is school like baseball?

The bell strikes one, two, three — and you're out!

Why did the baseball team sign up a two-headed monster?

To play double-headers.

What is the difference between a boy who is late for dinner and a baseball hit over the fence?

One runs home; the other is a home run.

What is the difference between a baseball player and a vampire?

One bats flies, the other flies bats.

What is the best way to get rid of flies?
Get good outfielders.

How can you make a fly ball?
Hit him with a bat.

Why was the piano tuner hired to play on the baseball team?

Because he had perfect pitch.

What song did the baseball player hum while he waited on third base?

"There's no place like home."

5. SCIENCE FOR DUMMIES

What did the robot say when it ran out of electricity?

"AC come, AC go."

What do you get when a robot's wires are reversed?

A lot of backtalk.

Why did the robot go to a psychiatrist?
It had a screw loose.

When is a robot like a surgeon?
When it operates on batteries.

What kind of doctor operates on Styrofoam robots?

A plastic surgeon.

What did the little electric robot say to its mother?

"I love you watts and watts."

What snacks should you serve robots at parties?

Assorted nuts.

Why did the scientist study electricity?

He wanted to keep up with current events.

What did the scientist get when she crossed an electric eel and a sponge?

Shock absorbers.

How did the scientist fix the robot gorilla?
With a monkey wrench.

What did the scientist get when he crossed
an old car and a gorilla?
A greasy monkey.

What would you get if you crossed a
breakfast drink and a monkey?
An orangu-tang.

What would you get if you crossed a stone
and a shark?
Rockjaws.

What would you get if you crossed a
Martian, a skunk, and an owl?
*An animal that stinks to high heaven and
doesn't give a hoot.*

What is the most educated thing in the
scientist's laboratory?
*A thermometer, because it has so many
degrees.*

When is it best to buy a thermometer?
In the winter, when it is lower.

How do you use a thermometer to find the height of a building?

Lower the thermometer on a string from the top of the building to the ground. Then measure the length of the string.

Why did the scientist throw the thermometer out of the laboratory on a hot day?

He wanted to see the temperature drop.

What mysterious thing did the scientist see in the skillet?

An unidentified frying object.

What would you get if you crossed a parrot and an elephant?

Something that tells everything it remembers.

What do you get if you cross a parrot and an army man?

A parrot-trooper.

What would you get if you crossed a parrot and a bumblebee?

An animal that talks all the time about how busy it is.

What would you get if you crossed a parrot and a canary?

A bird that knows both the words and the music.

What did the scientist get when he crossed a cat and a parrot?

A purr-a-keet.

What does it mean when a barometer falls?

That whoever nailed it up didn't do such a good job.

What would you get if you crossed the Invisible Man and a cow?

Vanishing cream.

What dog likes to hang around scientists?
A laboratory retriever.

Why didn't the scientist need a pocket calculator?

Because he already knew how many pockets he had.

What did the scientist get when he made an exact duplicate of Texas?

A clone star state.

What did the scientist get when he crossed a chicken and a cow?

Roost beef.

What is the difference between electricity and lightning?

You have to pay for electricity.

If lightning strikes an orchestra, who is most likely to get hit?

The conductor.

What is yellow and goes "hmmmm"?
An electric lemon.

What is yellow and long and always points north?
A magnetic banana.

What would you get if you crossed a banana and a bell?
A banana you can peel more than once.

What would you get if you crossed a sheep and a banana?
A baa-nana.

What would you get if you crossed a banana and a banana?
A pair of slippers.

Why don't bananas ever get lonely?
Because they go around in bunches.

84

What kind of typewriter does Count
Dracula use in his laboratory?
One that types blood.

What would you get if you crossed a
porcupine and an alarm clock?
A stickler for punctuality.

What did the scientist get when he crossed a clock and a rooster?

An alarm cluck.

What's the quickest way to make oil boil?
Add the letter "B."

What did the scientist get when he crossed
a chicken and a cement truck?
A hen that lays sidewalks.

What can you find in the center of gravity?
The letter "V."

Why can't you trust the law of gravity?
Because it always lets you down.

What weighs more – a pound of lead or a
pound of feathers?
They weigh the same – one pound.

What can you measure that has no length,
width, or thickness?
The temperature.

What did the scientist get when he crossed a frog and a soft drink?
Croak-a-cola.

What did the scientist get when he crossed an egg and a soft drink?
Yolk-a-cola.

The scientist invented a liquid that would dissolve anything it touched. He couldn't sell his invention, however. Why?
There was nothing in which he could put the liquid.

What happened when the scientist fell into the lens grinding machine?
He made a spectacle of himself.

What is H, I, J, K, L, M, N, O?
The formula for water — H to O.

What is the most important rule in
chemistry?
Never lick the spoon.

How is an airplane like an atom bomb?
One drop and you're dead.

What did the scientist write on the robot's tombstone?

"*RUST IN PEACE.*"

Who was the first nuclear scientist in history?

Eve — She knew all about atom (Adam).

Why did the scientist keep talking about the atom bomb?

He didn't want to drop the subject.

What do nuclear scientists argue about?

Whether splitting the atom was a wisecrack.

What is an atomic scientist's favorite snack?

Fission chips.

What is a hydrogen bomb?

Something that makes molehills out of mountains.

6. FUN FOOD

What snacks should you serve computer scientists at parties?

A byte of everything.

What kind of gum do chickens chew?

Chicklets.

What's the difference between a stupid person and a pizza?

One is easy to cheat and the other is cheesy to eat.

How many chickens does it take to serve
ten people?

*Chickens aren't good at serving. Better get
waiters and waitresses.*

How do you make an elephant sandwich?
First, get a very large loaf of bread...

Is chicken soup good for your health?
Not if you're a chicken.

How do you know that chickens love money?
They are always going, "Buck-buck! Buck-buck!"

What has bread on both sides and frightens easily.
A chicken sandwich.

What do dogs put on their pizza?
Mutts-arella.

What do ants put on their pizza?
Ant-chovies.

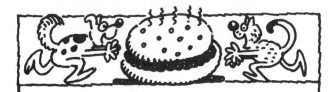

WHAT DO YOU LIKE WITH YOUR HAMBURGERS?

What do computer scientists like with their hamburgers?
Chips.

What do musicians like with their hamburgers?
Piccolos (pickle-o's).

What do spiders like with their hamburgers?
French flies.

What do cats put on their hamburgers?
Mouse-tard.

Why couldn't the hamburger talk?
The catsup got its tongue.

Is it a good idea to eat hamburgers on an empty stomach?
No, it's neater to eat them on a plate.

What music do young hamburgers like to listen to?
Rock 'n roll.

What's a burger's all-time favorite movie director?
Sizzle B. De Mille.

What does a lion eat when he goes to a restaurant?
The waiter.

What is the best thing to eat in a bathtub?
A sponge cake.

What do witches eat at cookouts?
Halloweenies (hollow wienies).

What smells best at a barbecue?
  A pickle holding its breathe.

Where do you put a very smart hot dog?
  On the honor roll.

How do you make a hot dog roll?
  Tilt your plate.

What is the best way to talk to a hot dog?
  Be frank.

What is a hot dog's favorite song?
  "Franks for the memory..."

What did the hot dog say when it won the race?
  "I'm a wiener!"

What is green and red all over?
  A pickle holding its breath.

What is a geologist's favorite dessert?
  Marble cake.

What sweets do geologists like?
  Rock candy.

What does the funniest kid in camp have for breakfast?
Cream of Wit.

What do cowboys put on their pancakes?
Maple stirrup.

What did Mary have at the cookout?
Everyone knows that Mary had a little lamb.

Why did the frog like French fries?
Because it was a pota-toad.

What has four legs and flies?
A picnic table.

What kind of ant can break a picnic table with one blow?
A gi-ant.

What do ghouls drink at picnics?
  Ice-ghoul lemonade.

What do frogs drink at picnics?
  Crock-a-cola.

What do dogs drink at picnics?
  Pupsi-cola.

7. HAVING A WONDERFUL TIME

Why is "H" the most popular letter of the alphabet?

It is the start of every holiday.

Why is it so hard to do nothing all summer?

Because you can't stop to rest.

Where does a Brontosaurus go for vacation?

To the dino-shore.

When are you most likely to dream about going away for the summer?
When you're asleep.

What is grey and wet and vacations in Florida?
A melted penguin.

What would you get if you crossed a bunch of bones and a week in Florida?
A skele-tan.

Why do skeletons always vacation alone?
Because they have no-body to go with.

Where do fish go for vacation?
Finland.

Where do songbirds go for vacation?
The Canary Islands.

What's black and white and hates to be touched?

A zebra just back from the beach.

Why is a cat on the beach like Christmas?

It has sandy claws (Santa Claus).

What is heavier in the summer than in the winter?

Traffic to the beach.

What did Cinderella wear when she went to the beach?

Glass flippers.

Where do race cars go swimming?

In the car pool.

Where do phantoms go swimming?

At the sea ghost.

Where do mummies go swimming?
In the Dead Sea.

What game do you play with fish?
Carps and robbers.

What do you get if a bunch of thieves
dives into the swimming pool?

A crime wave.

Why aren't elephants allowed in the
swimming pool?

Because they can't keep their trunks up.

Why did the tire need a vacation?
It couldn't take the pressure anymore.

Why did the three little pigs go on vacation?
Because their father was a boar.

Why isn't the moon a good place to go on vacation?
It lacks atmosphere.

Where do zombies go on vacation?
Club Dead.

Where does Lassie go on vacation?
Collie-fornia.

What is tan and has four legs and a trunk?
A mouse coming back from vacation.

What do octopuses take on camping trips?
Tent-acles.

How do you fix a torn tepee?
Apache here, Apache there.

Can you make a fire with one stick?
Yes, if it's a match.

What would you get if you crossed a
rabbit and a stand-up comic?

A funny bunny that walks on its hind legs.

What is the difference between a rabbit that runs three miles a day and a so-so comedian?

One is a fit bunny, the other is a bit funny.

When are boxers like comedians?

When they have you in stitches.

What would you get if you crossed a banana and a clown?

Peels of laughter.

What ducks crack jokes?

Wise quackers.

How are comedians like surgeons?

They are both cut-ups.

What's a comedian's favorite motorcycle?

A Yama-haha.

A hiker went without sleep for seven days and wasn't tired. How come?
He slept at night.

How did Barbie help the chicken with its part in the camp play?
Barbie cued the chicken.

Where do you send a shoe in the summer?
To boot camp.

What do you call someone with a big red nose and purple hair who takes a plane from New York to Alaska?
A passenger.

What do you call a father who takes a plane to the North Pole?
A cold pop.

Why isn't an elephant allowed on a plane?
Because his trunk won't fit under the seat.

How do you get a mouse to fly?
Buy it an airline ticket.

How do dogs travel?
By mutt-a-cycle.

What is big and hairy and travels 1,200 miles an hour?

King Kongcorde.

Where do pilots keep their personal things?

In air pockets.

What people travel the most?

Romans.

What people travel the fastest?

Russians.

Why don't people visit Transylvania?

Because it is a terror-tory.

What egg travels to unknown places?

An eggs-plorer.

How do mice find their way when they travel?

With rod-ent maps.

Where do people leave their dogs when they go on vacation?

At the arf-anage (orphanage).

What's the difference between a dog with fleas and a person going on vacation?

One is going to itch and the other is itching to go.

HOW DO THEY TRAVEL?

How do rabbits travel?
 By hareplane.

How does King Kong travel?
 By hairyplane.

How do barbers travel?
 By hairplane.

How do pizza pies travel?
 By pie-cycle.

How do witches travel when they
don't have a broom?
 They witch-hike.

Where do wolves stay when they travel?
In a Howl-iday Inn.

What always follows a wolf when it travels?
Its tail.

What boat takes dentists on short trips?
The Tooth Ferry.

Why is travel by boat the cheapest way of getting around?

Because boats run on water.

When does a boat show affection?

When it hugs the shore.

What vegetable is dangerous to have in a boat?

A leek (leak).

What would you get if you crossed a lake in a boat that had a leak in it?

About halfway.

What happens when you hike across a stream and a river?

Your feet get wet.

How do robots cross a lake?
In a row-bot.

What do frogs wear on their feet in summer?

Open toad shoes.

What did the hiker say when he ran into a
porcupine?
   "Ouch!"

What kind of singers do you find in
Yellowstone National Park?
Bear-itones.

How do bears walk?
In their bear feet.

8. ARE WE HAVING FUN YET?

What did the hiker say after being on safari for one week?

"Safari so good."

What did the hiker yell when he saw the avalanche?

"Here come the Rolling Stones!"

What musical key do you hear when a race car speeds through a coal mine?

A-flat miner (minor).

What musical instruments are best for catching fish?

Castanets.

What would you get if you crossed a sweet potato and a jazz musician?

Yam sessions.

What kind of music do you hear when you throw a stone into the lake?

Plunk rock.

What kind of car does a rich rock star drive?

A rock-n-Rolls Royce.

Why shouldn't you hit a famous composer?
He might hit you Bach.

Who leads a duck orchestra?
The con-duck-tor.

Why do so many orchestras have bad names?
Because they don't know how to conduct themselves.

What do you get when you cross a bag of cement, a stone, and a radio?

Hard rock music.

How is an actor in a hit show like a hockey player?

One sticks with a play, the other plays with a stick.

What sport is like a perfect score in the Olympics?

Tennis (ten is).

Why are waiters like tennis players?

They both have to know how to serve.

What is the difference between a tennis racket and a doughnut?

You can't dunk a tennis racket in a glass of milk.

Do vampires play tennis?
  No, they prefer bat-minton.

What is the difference between a prince
and a tennis ball?
  *One is heir to the throne, the other is thrown
  to the air.*

Why weren't tennis players allowed in summer camp?

Because they made too much of a racket (racquet).

Why are mountain climbers curious?

Because they always want to take another peak (peek).

Why didn't the mountain climber hurt himself when he fell off the cliff?

Because he was wearing a light fall suit.

How can you climb Mount Everest without getting tired?

Be born on top.

If you go on a trek through the desert, what should you take along?

A thirst-aid kit.

If you were on a trek in the Sahara Desert,
where would you get milk?

From the drome-dary (dairy).

Who is boss in the dairy?

The big cheese.

Why can't you play hide-and-seek with baby chickens?
Because they're always peeping.

Where do cows go to see art?
Moo-seums.

Why don't scarecrows have fun?
Because they are such stuffed shirts.

Why is Count Dracula like the Frankenstein monster?
Neither can play Ping-Pong.

Why didn't the cow want to play Ping-Pong?
She wasn't in the moo-d.

What did one toad say to the other toad?
"One more game of leapfrog — and I'll croak!"

What were the chickens doing in the
health club?

Eggs-ercising.

What is green, has big eyes, and eats like a pig?

Kermit the Hog.

What is green, has big eyes, and is hard to see through?

Kermit the Fog.

What does a mechanical frog say?

"Robot, robot!"

What wallows in mud and carries colored eggs?

The Easter Piggie.

Why can't you play games with pigs?
Because they hog the ball.

When do pigs give their girlfriends
presents?
On Valen-swine's Day.

What did the executioner do at
Christmas?

He went sleighing (slaying).

What is the difference between little kids
at Christmas and werewolves?

*Werewolves have claws on their fingers; little
kids at Christmas have claws (Claus) on
their minds.*

What would you get if you crossed a
reindeer and a firefly?
Rudolph the Red-Nosed Firefly.

What did the hen do when it saw the large
order of Kentucky Fried Chicken?
It kicked the bucket.

What would you get if you crossed some
chocolate candy and a sheep?
A Hershey baa.

What lives on the bottom of the sea and is
popular at Easter?
An oyster egg.

How can you drop an egg ten feet without
breaking it?
*Drop it eleven feet. It won't break for the
first ten.*

What does a parrot say on the Fourth of July?

"Polly wants a firecracker!"

What did one firecracker say to the other firecracker?

"My pop is bigger than your pop."

Where do geologists go to relax?
Rock concerts.

What is a geologist's favorite lullaby?
  "Rock-a-bye, Baby."

How do you make notes out of stone?
  Rearrange the letters.

Who is brown and hairy and fights forest
fires?
  A suntanned forest ranger who needs a shave.

How do hikers cross a patch of poison
ivy?
  They itch hike.

How do hikers dress on cold mornings?
  Quickly.

Two campers were playing checkers. They
played five games and each won the same
number of games. How is this possible?
  They played different people.

What would you get if you crossed a
chicken and a television set?
   A TV show that lays eggs.

Why are you like a shrub after a long hike?

Because you're bushed.

What is the worst thing you're likely to find in the camp kitchen?

The food.

How do they count muffins in the camp kitchen?

They have a roll call.

How do you greet a web-footed bird?

"What's up, duck?"

What is the difference between a football player and a duck?

You'll find one in a huddle and the other in a puddle.

How can you tell if there is a football team in your bathtub?

It's hard to close the shower curtain.

What did the football say to the player?
"I get a kick out of you."

What did the football say after the player
threw it?
"You send me!"

What did the helmet say to the football
player?
"You're putting me on!"

How do we know that football referees are
happy?
Because they whistle while they work.

Who are the happiest people at the game?
The cheer leaders.

Which football player wears the biggest
helmet?
The one with the biggest head.

Would you rather have a 300-pound football player attack you or a 300-pound wrestler?

I'd rather have them attack each other.

What did the football player say when he was hit by lightning?

"Got to glow now!"

9. BACK TO MOTHER NATURE

Which is lighter – the sun or the earth?
The sun, because it rises every morning.

Why is the moon like a dollar?
Because it has four quarters.

How many pieces of string does it take to reach the moon?
One, if it is long enough.

When is the moon heaviest?
When it is full.

Who was the first man in space?
The man in the moon.

Why did Humpty Dumpty have a great fall?

To make up for a boring summer.

Whose fault will it be if California falls into the ocean?

San Andreas fault.

What do you call a geologist who doesn't hear anything?

Stone deaf.

What happens to a small stone when it works up its courage?

It becomes a little boulder (bolder).

When are geologists unpopular?

When they are fault-finders.

When are geologists unhappy?

When people take them for granite.

What does a geologist have for breakfast?
Rock-n-roll.

What color is the wind?
Blew.

What gets harder to catch the faster you run?
Your breath.

What runs, but never gets out of breath?
Water.

What goes through water but doesn't get wet?
A ray of light.

How do you open the Great Lakes?
With the Florida Keys.

Why are there bridges over water?
So people won't step on the fishes.

Where is a lake deepest?
On the bottom.

What does one raindrop say to the other raindrop?
"My plop is bigger than your plop."

What is the difference between the North Pole and the South Pole?

All the difference in the world.

What did one pile of sand say to the other pile of sand?

"Dune anything tonight?"

Why did the river bend?

Because it saw the waterfall.

Where do rivers sleep?

In river beds.

When does a river flood?

When it gets too big for its bridges.

What body of water is a famous spy?

James Pond.

What doesn't get wetter – no matter how much it rains?

The ocean.

What's the most romantic part of the ocean?

The spot where buoy meets gull.

What did the ocean say to the beach?
"I'm not shore."

Who does the ocean date?
It goes out with the tide.

How do you cut the ocean in two?
With a sea-saw.

Why is the ocean so grouchy?
Because it has crabs all over its bottom.

What lives in the water and takes you anywhere you want to go?

A taxi crab.

When is the ocean friendliest?
When it waves.

Why did the ocean roar at the ships?
Because they crossed it so many times.

Why was the ocean arrested?
Because it beat upon the shore.

What do two oceans say when they meet
after many years?
"Long time no sea."

What do you call a long series of
hurricane names?
A gust (guest) list.

A camper fell out of a canoe into the
middle of the lake. He neither swam nor
sank. How could that be?
He floated.

What did one magnet say to the other magnet?

"You attract me."

What did one volcano say to the other volcano?

"I lava you."

What do you call it when Mother Nature crosses an earthquake and a forest fire?
Shake and Bake.

What's the longest distance you can see?
Down a road with telephone poles, because then you can see from pole to pole.

What is "mean temperature"?
Twenty degrees below zero when you don't have long underwear.

What is the best kind of letter to read on a hot day?
Fan mail.

What animal cools you off on a hot day?
A pup-sicle.

What makes bluebirds blue?
Their blue genes (jeans).

Who wears a black cape, flies through the night and wants to drink your flood?

A mosquito in a black cape.

What is green, has big eyes, and lives all alone in the pond?

Hermit the Frog.

What goes "Dit-dot-dot-croak, dit-dot-dot-croak"?

Morse toad.

What do you call a fat tree limb?
  A porky twig.

What is the smartest tree in the forest?
  Albert Pinestein.

What is a tree's favorite drink?
  Root beer.

A Boy Scout climbed a tall pine tree to gather some acorns. He tried all morning, but couldn't get any. Why not?
  Acorns don't grow on pine trees. They grow on oak trees.

What lives in the forest, is green, and pecks on trees?
  Woody Wood Pickle.

10. BIRDS OF A FEATHER

What kind of geese come from Portugal?
Portu-geese.

Why did the hen sit on the axe?
She thought she could hatch-it.

Why did the muddy chicken cross the road twice?

Because she was a dirty double-crosser.

Why is a black chicken smarter than a white one?

A black chicken can lay white eggs, but a white chicken can't lay black eggs.

Which side of a chicken has the most feathers?

The outside.

Where can you find out more about chickens?

In a hen-cyclopedia.

Where can you find out more about ducks?

In a duck-tionary.

What book tells you about all the different kinds of owls?

Who's Whoo.

Why was the owl the hit of the talent show?

He was a h-owl!

What do you call it when it rains chickens and ducks?

Foul (fowl) weather.

What was the near-sighted chicken doing in the farmer's garden?

She was sitting on an eggplant.

What does a Spanish farmer say to his chickens?

"Oh, lay!" (Olé)

Why couldn't the chicken find her eggs?

She mislaid them.

What has four legs, is very long, and goes "quack, quack"?

A ducks-hund.

Why did the hens go on strike?

They refused to work for chicken feed.

Why did the hen sit down in the middle of the tennis court?
She wanted to lay it on the line.

What would you get if you crossed a chicken and an old timepiece?
A grandfather cluck.

How do chickens get out of their shell?
They eggs-it.

How can you make an egg run faster?
You egg it on.

11. HEALTHY, WEALTHY, & WEIRD

What doctor treats his patients like animals?

A vet.

When is a vet busiest?

When it rains cats and dogs.

When it rains cats and dogs, what does a vet step into?

Poodles.

What is worse than an elephant with an earache?

A giraffe with a sore throat.

Does a giraffe get a sore throat when its feet get wet?

Yes, but not until two weeks later.

What's the difference between a photocopier and a virus?

One makes facsimilies; the other makes sick families.

What's the difference between a bus driver and a cold?

One knows the stops; the other stops the nose.

What do they do with a cowboy whose voice is really hoarse?

They put a saddle on it.

Why did the doctor pour oil on his hands?

He wanted to be a smooth operator.

What does a polite doctor say when he is about to operate?

"May I cut in?"

Why can't you believe what doctors say?

Because they make MD (empty) promises.

How long should doctors practice medicine?

Until they get it right.

What is a medicine dropper?

A doctor with greasy fingers.

What did the doctor use to fix a broken heart?

Ticker tape.

What was the plumber doing in the operating room?

He was a drain surgeon.

Why do surgeons wear masks during operations?
So that, if they make a mistake, no one will know who did it.

Why did the dog see the doctor?
Because a stitch in time saves canine.

How can you tell when Count Dracula is catching cold?
From his coffin (coughin').

What happens when corn catches cold?
It gets an earache.

Where does a sneeze usually point?
At-choo (at you)!

What kind of paper is most like a sneeze?
A tissue.

What is the difference between a person with a cold and a strong wind?
One blows a sneeze; the other blows a breeze.

What is red, white, and blue, and convenient when you sneeze?
A hanky doodle dandy.

What should you say when the Statue of
Liberty sneezes?
  "God bless America."

You can never catch cold going up in an elevator. True or false?

True. You come down with a cold. You come up with a cure.

What would happen if you swallowed a dress?

You'd have a frock (frog) in your throat.

What sickness can't you talk about until it's cured?

Laryngitis.

What sickness did Bruce Lee get?

Kung flu.

What's the difference between a boxer and a person with a cold?

A boxer knows his blows; a person with a cold blows his nose.

What's the difference between ammonia and pneumonia?

Ammonia comes in bottles; pneumonia comes in chests.

What did one elevator say to the other elevator?

"I think I'm coming down with something."

How do you feel if you have a sore throat and fleas?

Hoarse and buggy.

What's the difference between a hill and a pill?

A hill is hard to get up; a pill is hard to get down.

What's the difference between a sick sailor and a blind man?

One can't go to sea; the other can't see to go.

What has 18 legs, red spots, and catches flies?

A baseball team with the measles.

Why is a catcher's glove like the measles?

Both are catching.

What's the best game to play when you've got the measles?

Hide-and-sick.

What game is dangerous to your mental health?

Marbles – if you lose them.

When was medicine first mentioned in the Bible?

It was when Moses received the two tablets.

What do you give an elk with indigestion?

Elk-a-Seltzer.

What did the farmer use to cure his sick hog?

Oinkment (ointment).

How is medicine packaged for astronauts?

In space capsules.

Why did the silly kid jump up and down?

The medicine label said, "Shake well."

Why did the silly kid swing on the chandelier?

Because her doctor told her to get some light exercise.

What do doctors give elephants to calm them down?

Trunk-quilizers.

How much did the elephant have to pay to the psychiatrist?

A hundred dollars for the hour and six hundred dollars for the couch.

Why did the wrestler go to the psychiatrist?
He couldn't get a grip on himself.

Why did the fencer go to the psychiatrist?
Because of her duel (dual) personality.

When someone comes to your door, what is the polite thing to do?
Vitamin (invite him in).

What contains the most vitamins?
A health food store.

What bee is necessary to your health?
Vitamin B.

On what day do you moan the most?
On Moan-day.

What kind of fish is in charge of an operating room?

The head sturgeon.

What would you do if you found yourself with water on the knee, water on the elbow, and water on the brain?

Turn off the shower.

What happened when the plastic surgeon stood too close to the fire?

He melted.

Who flies on a broom and carries a medicine bag?
  A witch doctor.

What is the best way to get rid of demons?
  Exorcise (exercise).

What kind of physician comes from Cairo?
  A chiropractor.

What did the tree say to the tree surgeon?
  "Leaf me alone!"

Why don't anteaters have infections?
  Because they're filled with anty-bodies.

What gets 25 miles to a gallon of plasma?
  A bloodmobile.

What should you do with a sick boat?
  Take it to the dock (doc).

What does a doctor do with a sick
zeppelin?

He tries to helium.

What's the difference between a sick person and seven days?

One is a weak one; the other is one week.

What's the difference between a dressmaker and a nurse?

One cuts the dresses; the other dresses the cuts.

Where is the best place to build offices for opticians and optometrists?

On a sight for sore eyes.

How is an eye doctor like a teacher?

They both test the pupils.

What do eye doctors sing when they test you?

"Oh, say can you see ..."

What did Old MacDonald see on the eye chart?

E-I-E-I-O.

What's the difference between a person with a terrible toothache and a rainy day?

One is roaring with pain; the other is pouring with rain.

Why do elephants in Alabama have to go
to the dentist so often?

*Because in Alabama Tuscaloosa (tusks are
looser).*

What is the best time to see a dentist?
Tooth-hurty (2:30).

Where does a rat go when it has a sore tooth?
To the rodent-ist.

What does a dentist say when you knock on his door?
"Gum on in!"

What did the tooth say to the dentist?
"Fill 'er up!"

What does the dentist do on his yacht?
Off-shore drilling.

When do most of your dollars go to the orthodontist?
When you have buck teeth.

12. GET WELL SOON!

Why did the chicken see the doctor?
It had people pox.

Why did the math book see the doctor?
It had problems.

What is grey, carries flowers, and cheers you when you're sick?
A get-well-ephant.

What relative will help you when you have an infection?
Anti-biotics.

WHAT DO THEY
COME DOWN WITH?

What do dancers come down with?
Ballet-aches.

What do chimneys come down with?
The flu.

What does grass come down with?
Hay fever.

What do cabbages come down with?
Headaches.

What animal do you feel like when you
have a fever?
A little otter (hotter).

Why don't rabbits multiply when they
have colds?
Because they can't breed (breathe).

WHAT DO THEY COME DOWN WITH?

What do beekeepers come down with?
Hives.

What do motorcycle riders come down with?
Vroom-atism.

What does Mickey Mouse come down with?
Disney spells.

What do video cassettes come down with?
Tapeworms.

Where do they take care of sick parrots?
In a polyclinic.

Where do they send sick kangaroos?
To the hop-ital.

Where do they send sick ponies?
To the horse-pital.

Where do they send sick librarians?
To the hush-pital.

What do they give the sick insects?
To the wasp-ital.

What medical condition helps you run faster?

Athlete's foot.

What is a foot doctor's favorite song?

"There's No Business Like Toe Business."

What kind of X-rays do foot doctors make?

Foot-ographs.

What do you get if you add 13 hospital patients and 13 hospital patients?

Twenty sicks (26).

Why did the nurse tiptoe past the medicine cabinet?

She didn't want to wake the sleeping pills.

How does a sick pig get to the hospital?

In a ham-bulance.

Why aren't vampires welcome at the
bloodmobile?
*Because they only want to make
withdrawals.*

Why wasn't the chicken allowed to visit
the hospital?
Because she fowled things up.

What would you get if your doctor
became a vampire?
More blood tests than ever.

What kind of music do you hear when the
nurse turns down your bed?
Sheet music.

What sign do you see in front of a dog
hospital?
No Barking Zone."

How did the patient get to the hospital so fast?

Flu.

Why do you lie down on a hospital bed?

Because you can't lie up.

What kind of alligator do you find in a hospital?

An illigator.

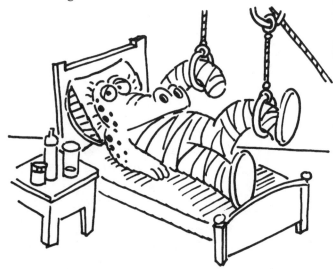

What has 15 letters, begins with an "A," ends with a "G," and means incredible pain?

"ARRRRRHHHHH-HHHG!"

Why do many mummies have high blood pressure?
Because they're so wound up.

What did the bed sheet say to the patient?
"Hold still – I've got you covered!"

Why were the bedcovers depressed?
Because the nurses turned them down.

Why did the doctor give up his practice?
He lost his patience.

When is it all right to belt a doctor?
When he gets in your car.

Why did the mother owl take her baby to the doctor?

Because it didn't give a hoot.

What do you tell a germ when it fools around?
"Don't bacilli!"

Why did the germ cross the microscope?
To get to the other side.

Which germ tastes best with pancakes?
Aunt Germ-ima.

What did one germ say to the other germ?
"You're making me sick."

Why do people with colds get plenty of exercise?
Their noses run.

Why was Whistler's mother in the hospital?
She went off her rocker.

Why did the turkey go to the hospital?
He had one foot in the grave-y.

What goes "Chit-chat, tick tock, boom-gong"?

A sick clock.

GRADUATING FROM
MEDICAL SCHOOL

What do you call a duck who
graduates from medical school?
"Duck-tor."

What do you call a dog who
graduates from medical school?
"Dog-tor."

What do you call a squid that
graduates from medical school?
"Doc-topus."

What mental illness does Santa suffer from?

Claustrophobia.

What nationality is Santa Claus?

North Polish.

When do most doctors graduate from medical school?

In Doc-tober.

What do you have if your head feels hot, your feet are cold, and you see spots in front of your eyes?

You probably have a polka-dotted sock over your head.

WHAT'S THE PROBLEM?

What was Ronald McDonald's problem?
Fallen arches.

What was the Olympic athlete's problem?
Slipped discus.

What problems do you get from eating too much?
You get thick (sick) to your stomach.

What did the surgeon say to the patient as
he sewed him up?

"That's enough out of you!"

13. FIGHTING WORDS

Who tells people where to get off and gets away with it?

A bus driver.

Who tells people where to go and gets away with it?

A travel agent.

How do cattle defend themselves?
They use cow-a-ti (karate).

How does a skunk defend itself?
Instinct.

Why did the karate expert wear a black belt?
To keep his pants up.

What tree is a karate champion?
  Spruce Lee.

What is small, round and green, and
knows karate?
  Bruce Pea.

What do you get when a pea picks a fight with a boxer?
A black-eyed pea.

How do you shake hands with a judo expert?
Very carefully.

Why did the matador take judo lessons?
He wanted to learn how to throw the bull.

On the door of a school was a sign that read:

PLEASE DON'T KNOCK BEFORE ENTERING

What kind of school was it?
A karate school.

What would you get if a pig learned karate?

Pork chops.

What was the artist doing in the boxing ring?

They needed him in case the fight ended in a draw.

What is the difference between a winter day and a boxer who is down for the count?

One is cold out, and other is out cold.

The boxer was knocked out. What number did they use to revive him?

They brought him 2.

Why is a boxer's hand never larger than eleven inches long?

If it were twelve inches long, it would be a foot.

Why couldn't the boxer light the fire?

Because he lost all his matches.

What is the difference between a nail and a bad boxer?

One is knocked in; the other is knocked out.

Why did the boxer hit the grandfather clock?

The clock struck first.

Why did the clock strike first?

Because it was ticked off.

What would you get if a hen stepped into
the ring with the heavyweight champion
of the world?

Creamed chicken.

What kind of potatoes would you get if you stepped into the ring with the heavyweight champion of France?

French fright (fried).

What happened when the watch fought the heavyweight champion?

The watch took a licking, but kept on ticking.

Why is boxing the world champion like singing in a barbershop quartet?

Because if you don't look sharp, you'll be flat.

Why did the mother skunk take her baby to the doctor?

Because it was out of odor.

What four letters can you say to someone who has been in the ring with a professional wrestler?

R-U-O-K.

Where does a big, mean, 300-pound wrestler sit, when he gets on a bus?

Anywhere he wants to.

Who is the best fencer in the ocean?
The swordfish.

How do you tell a big, mean wrestler from a bunny rabbit?
You don't tell a big, mean wrestler anything.

What did the fencer say when he was defeated?

"Curses! Foiled again!"

What does a fencing master do at twelve o'clock?

He goes to lunge.

Why do mosquitoes bother people most late at night?

Because mosquitoes like a little bite before they go to sleep.

When are mosquitoes most annoying?

When they get under your skin.

Did you hear about the mosquito who went to Hollywood?

All she could get were bit parts.

What geometric figure is the most dangerous?
A firing line.

How do people feel after they've been shot by a six-shooter?
Holier.

How do you make a mothball?
Hit it.

What does a tick attack?
A tick attacks a toe (Tic-tac-toe).

Why was the insect kicked out of the national park?
Because it was a litterbug.

What did the lettuce say to the farmer?
"Lettuce alone!"

What two vegetables fight crime?
Beetman and Radish.

Why was the lamb punished?
Because it was baaaa-d!

14. THE NOT-SO-GREAT OUTDOORS

What is a mile high and spins?
A mountain top.

How do mountains hear?
With mountaineers (mountain ears).

Where do scientists raise magnets?
In magnetic fields.

What is yellow and always helpful?
A Boy Scout banana.

What grows fast and goes camping?
A Boy Sprout.

What do you call a deer with no eyes?
No-eye-deer (no idea).

What do you call a deer wiith no eyes and
no legs?
Still no-eye-deer.

How do deer start a race?
They say, "Ready, set – DOE!"

Why did the horse sneeze?
It had a little colt.

What is the difference between a horse
and the weather?
One is reined up, the other rains down.

What would happen if black widow
spiders were as big as horses?
*If one bit you, you could ride it to the
hospital.*

When you are trying to tell a story around the campfire, why don't you want goats to be there?

Because they're always butting in.

What do you call a very large moose?
Enor-moose.

What is the hardest thing about learning
to ride wild horses?
The ground.

Why are wild horses rich?
They have a million bucks.

What do you get if you blow your hair
dryer down a rabbit hole?

Hot cross bunnies.

A horse was tied to a 15-foot rope, but he walked 30 feet. How come?

The rope wasn't tied to anything.

Why was the little horse unhappy?

Because its mother always said, "Neigh!"

How do you say goodbye to a horse?

You say, "I've got to whoa now!"

How does a farmer cut his grass?

With a lawn moo-er.

How did the farmer find his missing cow?

He tractor down.

Why do cows live in barns?

They're too big for birdhouses.

What cow lives in a haunted farmhouse?
Cow-nt Dracula.

What is the difference between a berry
farmer and a pirate?
*The farmer treasures his berries; the pirate
buries his treasures.*

How do gardeners start a race?
They say "Ready, set — sow!"

How do farmers start a race?
They say "Ready, set — hoe!"

What goes in one ear and out the other?
A worm in a cornfield.

Why did the farmer take a hammer to bed
with him?
So he could hit the hay.

Why do ranchers ride horses?
Because horses are too heavy to carry.

What do baby sweet potatoes sleep in?
  Their yammies.

What do you get when a football team
plays in your potato field?
  Mashed potatoes.

What tables grow on a farm?
  Vegetables.

What kind of pole do you have when five frogs sit on top of each other?

A toad-em pole.

What do you say when you meet a toad?

"Wart's new?"

Where do frogs shop?

Montgomery Wart.

Why are frogs so touchy?

Go near them and they croak.

What would you get if you crossed a rabbit and a frog?

A bunny ribbit.

What job did the frog take in the resort hotel?

Bell hop.

What animal uses a nutcracker?
A toothless squirrel.

How does a nut feel when a squirrel chews on it?

Nut so good.

What do you call a woodpecker with no beak?

A headbanger.

Why didn't the eagle get its hair wet when it went swimming?

It was a bald eagle.

What does an owl answer when you knock on its door?

"Whooooo is it?"

Why do owls call at night?

Because night rates are cheaper.

What detective stories do owls read?

Whoo-dunits.

How do we know that owls are smarter than chickens?

Have you ever heard of Kentucky Fried Owl?

What would you get if you crossed an owl
and a goat?
A hootenanny.

What do you say to an intelligent firefly?
"For a little fellow, you're very bright."

Why did the farmer put an umbrella over
the rabbit hutch?
He didn't want his hare to get wet.

What would you get if you crossed an
insect and a hare?
Bugs Bunny.

What did the boy firefly say to the girl firefly?
"I glow for you."

Two flies were in the camp kitchen. Which
one was the football player?
The one in the Sugar Bowl.

What time is it when the farmer looks at his bees?

Hive o'clock.

What do you call a young bee?

A babe-bee.

What is a bee's favorite song?

"Stinging in the Rain."

Why do bees hum?

Because they don't know the words.

What did the farmer get when he tried to reach the beehive?

A buzzy signal.

Why do bees have sticky hair?

Because there's honey on their combs.

Where do sheep go when they need a haircut?

To the baa-baa shop.

What is a sheep's favorite snack?
  A bah-loney sandwich.

Why don't sheep have enough money to go on vacation?
  The farmer is always fleecing them.

What is a fighter's favorite dog?
A boxer.

What is a bowler's favorite dog?
A setter.

What is a baseball player's favorite dog?
A good retriever that wears a muzzle, chases flies, and beats it for home when it sees the catcher.

What is a weightlifter's favorite dog?
A Siberian husky.

What is a chef's favorite dog?
A chow.

What is Hamlet's favorite dog?
A Great Dane.

Where do little dogs sleep when they go camping?

In pup tents.

What do you tell young dogs when they make noise outside your tent?

"Hush, puppies!"

Why didn't the witch like to sleep in a tent?

Because it didn't have a broom closet.

When does a camper go "Zzzz – meow – zzz – meow"?

When he's taking a catnap.

Why did the camper put his tent on the stove?

He wanted a home on the range.

What do people say about a mushroom who cracks great jokes?

"What a fungi!"

What is worse than having a snake in your sleeping bag?

Having two snakes in your sleeping bag.

What would you get if you crossed an animal from the Wild West and a duck?

Buffalo Bill.

What did the father buffalo say to his son when he went off to school?

"Bison!"

What do buffaloes celebrate every 100 years?

Their Bison-tennial.

What is the best thing to do if you find a
skunk in your sleeping bag?
Sleep somewhere else.

What fur do you get from a skunk?
As fur as possible.

What do skunks have that no other
animals have?
Baby skunks.

What did one skunk say to the other
skunk when they met a group of hikers in
the woods?
"Come — let us spray."

What would you get if you crossed a
skunk and a boomerang?
A smell you couldn't get rid of.

Which skunk smells the worst?
  The one with the cheapest perfume.

What would you get if you crossed a small bear and a skunk?
Winnie the Pooh.

What would you get if you crossed a small bear and a cow?
Winnie the Moo.

What is quicker than a fish?
The one who catches it.

How do you stop fish from smelling?
Hold their noses.

How do you communicate with a fish?
Drop it a line.

Why did the silly athlete bring a rod and reel to the football tryouts?
He heard they were looking for a tackle.

Why did Dr. Jekyll go to the beach?
To tan his hide (Hyde).

Why did Little Audrey tiptoe past the campers?

She didn't want to wake the sleeping bags.

What happened when the silly camper bought a sleeping bag?

He spent three weeks trying to wake it up.

How can you tell if there is an elephant in your sleeping bag?

By the smell of peanuts on his breath.

How do you make a bedroll?

Push it down a hill.

Why did the little boy put a frog in his sister's sleeping bag?

Because he couldn't find a snake.

How do moths swim?
  They do the butterfly.

How do babies swim?
  They do the crawl.

How can you tell when the ocean wants to meet you?

The tidal (tide'll) wave.

What did the banana say before it dived into the lake?

"I think I'll peel first."

How can you dive without getting wet?
  Go sky diving.

How do little kids get to use the swimming pool?
  They wade on line.

What do lawyers like to wear when they go swimming?
  Bathing suits.

What do lawyers wear when they go running?
  Briefs.

Why couldn't Batman go fishing?
  Because Robin ate all the worms.

What is a worm's favorite opera?
  Rigoletto (wriggle-etto).

What do you call a frightened scuba
diver?

Chicken of the Sea.

Where did the seahorse live?
In the barn-acle.

What do you say to someone who falls off his surfboard because he's showing off?
"Surf's you right!"

How do boaters start a race?
They say, "Ready, set — row!"

Gladys went swimming. She saw a big shark, but she wasn't afraid. Why not?
Because it was a man-eating shark.

What is worse than seeing a shark's fins?
Seeing its tonsils.

What do sharks call swimmers?
Dinner!

Why is the ocean so angry?
It's been crossed.

How does a river say goodbye?
"Got to flow now!"

How does the ocean say goodbye?
"I'll be sea-ing you!"

How do you say goodbye to the ocean?
You wave.

15. FAR OUT!

What did the Martian say when he landed in a field of weeds?

"Take me to your weeder."

What is soft, white, and comes from Mars?

Martian-mallows.

Where do Martians leave their spaceships?
At parking meteors.

What does the sun do when it gets tired?
   It sets a while.

How do you tune in to the sun?
   With a sun dial.

What travels around the earth all year
without using a drop of fuel?
   The moon.

Who really likes to be down and out?
   An airsick astronaut.

What is the secret of being a happy
astronaut?
   Never look down.

What is an astronaut's favorite meal?
   Launch.

Why do astronauts wear bullet-proof vests?

To protect themselves against shooting stars.

What do astronauts do when they get angry?

They blast off.

What do astronauts do when they get dirty?

They take a meteor shower.

How do Martians drink their tea?

From flying saucers.

What do you call a person who is crazy about going into space?

An astro-nut.

What do Martians do in space when they get thirsty?

They drink from the Big Dipper.

How do you arrange for a trip to Mars?

You planet (plan it).

How do you get to the Planet of the Apes?

By banana boat.

What is round and purple and orbits the sun?

The Planet of the Grapes.

What is the noisiest planet?
Saturn, because it has so many rings.

What do you call an astronaut who is afraid of heights?
A failure.

Why was the astronaut wrong when he landed on the moon and reported there was no life there?
There was – with him on it.

What did the astronaut get when the rocket fell on his foot?
Mistletoe.

Why did the astronaut lie on the bed before he blasted off?
He wanted to count down.

How do you put a baby astronaut to
sleep?

You rock-et.

What would you get if you crossed a 50-
foot Martian and a 300-pound chicken?

The biggest cluck in the solar system.

What is covered with ribbons and bows and comes from outer space?
A gift-wrapped Martian.

Where do Martians go swimming?
In the galaxies (galax-seas).

What do little astronauts get when they do
their homework?
Gold stars.

Why did the scientist pinch the waitress?
He wanted to see some flying saucers.

What would you get if you crossed a galaxy and a toad?
Star Warts.

16. DRIVING YOURSELF CRAZY

What looks like a snake, swims in water, and honks?

An automob-eel.

What kind of car do you drive in the fall?

An autumn-mobile.

What makes the road broad?

The letter "B."

What kind of car do rich cats drive?
  Cat-illacs.

What kind of car do rich steers drive?
  Cattle-acs.

CROSSING THE ROAD

Why did the chicken cross the road?
To get to the other side.

What was the farmer doing on the
other side of the road?
*Catching all the chickens who tried to
cross the road.*

What do you call a chicken that
crosses the road without looking
both ways?
Dead.

What has two arms, two wings, two tails,
three heads, three bodies, and eight legs?
A cowboy on horseback holding a chicken.

CROSSING THE ROAD

Why did the turkey cross the road?
It was the chicken's day off.

Why did the elephant cross the road?
To prove he wasn't chicken.

Why did the one-handed man cross the road?
To get to the second-hand shop.

Why did the surfer cross the road?
To get to the other tide.

What has fur on the outside and feathers on the inside?

A chicken in a mink coat.

What kind of running means walking?
Running out of gas.

What is the difference between the back light of a car and a short story?
One is a tail light; the other is a light tale.

What equipment is standard on a crying car?
Windshield weepers.

Why do cars have such bad memories?
Because things go in one gear and out the other.

What songs do automobiles sing?
Car tunes (cartoons).

Where do old Volkswagens end up?
In the Old Volks (folks) Home.

What kind of car do toads drive?
  Hop rods.

What is purple, very wrinkled, and goes
SLAM-SLAM-SLAM-SLAM?
  A four-door prune.

What would you get if you crossed an automobile, a dog, and a broom?

A car-pet sweeper.

How do you keep a dog from barking in the front seat of your car?

Make him sit in the back.

What is a good license plate for a sports car?

X L R 8.

What would you have if your car's motor was in flames?

A fire engine.

What would happen if a bunch of frogs sat in a no-parking zone?

They would get toad (towed) away.

What do you call an elephant hitchhiker?
A two-and-a-half-ton pickup.

What happened when the tire drove over
the nail?
The nail knocked it flat.

What kind of car is good for carrying bunny rabbits?

A hutch-back.

What kind of car do hound dogs drive?

Houndas.

What do you call a car thief who steals Hondas?

A Honda-taker (undertaker).

What do Honda owners wear close to their skin?

Honda-wear.

What is the funniest car on the road?

A Jolkswagen.

Why did the motorist shoot his car?

He wanted to kill the motor.

CROSSING THE ROAD

Why did the duck cross the road?
*Because the chicken retired and moved
to Florida.*

Why did the otter cross the road?
To get to the otter side.

Why did the turtle cross the road?
To get to the Shell station.

Why did the goose cross the road?
Because the light was green.

Why did the man put a rabbit in his gas tank?

Because he only used the car for short hops.

CROSSING THE ROAD

Why did the rabbit cross the road?
To get to the hopping mall.

Why did the cow cross the road?
To see its fodder.

Why did Dr. Jekyll cross the road?
To get to the other Hyde.

What was Count Dracula doing on the road?
Looking for the main artery.

What has four wheels and roars down the highway?

A lion on a skateboard.

A man drove 2,000 miles with his family without knowing he had a flat tire. How come?

It was his spare tire that was flat.

What is the laziest part of a car?

The wheels — they're always tired.

What did one car say to the other car?

"Well, strip my gears and call me shiftless!"

What did one car muffler say to the other car muffler?

"Boy, am I exhausted!"

What did the jack say to the car?

"Can I give you a lift?"

What has cities without houses, rivers without water, and forests without trees?

A road map.

CROSSING THE ROAD

Why did the dinosaur cross the road?
Because in those days they didn't have chickens.

Why was the elephant on the road?
Trying to trip the ants.

Why did the atoms cross the road?
I was time to split.

What would you get if you crossed the road with a bag of money?
Mugged!

What do police use to patrol the seashore?
A squid car.

What is the last thing a trapeze flyer wants
to be?
The fall guy.

What goes "peckety-peck" and points north?

A magnetic chicken.

What do you say to a hitchhiking frog?

"Hop in!"

What do you say to a hitchhiking angel?

"Harp in!"

17. PLAYING AROUND

When was baseball first mentioned in the Bible?

In the opening words: "In the big inning (beginning)."

In which inning is the score always 0–0?

In the OP-inning (opening).

What inning is it when the Frankenstein monster steps up to bat?

The fright-inning (frightening).

What is the difference between a slow ball and a fast ball?

The difference between a lump on the head and a fractured skull.

Why did the pitcher let the baseball player walk?

He was too tired to run.

What would you get if you crossed a pitcher and the Invisible Man?

Pitching like no one has ever seen.

How are baseball players like song writers?

They're both interested in big hits.

Why didn't the Confederate soldier want to go to the ball game?

He heard the Yankees were playing.

What happens when baseball players get old?

They go batty.

Which three Rs must every cheerleader know?

RAH! RAH! RAH!

What color is a cheerleader?
Yell-ow.

What do cheerleaders like to drink?
Root beer.

What flavor ice cream do cheerleaders
like best?
Rahs-berry.

What do cheerleaders have for breakfast?
Cheer-ios.

Why do elephants wear blue sneakers?
Because white ones get dirty too fast.

Why did the elephant go to the gym
wearing Adidas?
His Reeboks were in the wash.

Where did the Loch Ness monster put on its sneakers?

In the loch-er room.

What kind of bell doesn't ring?
A dumbbell.

What do you call it when a weightlifter
drops his dumbbell?
A power failure.

What happened when the weightlifter took
a bath?
The police made him bring it back.

What shellfish lifts weights?
Mussels.

What grows on trees and can lift
tremendous weights?
Hercu-leaves.

Why did the chicken lift weights?
She needed the eggs-ercise.

How do witches feel when they play croquet?

Wicket.

How can you tell witch twins apart?

It's not easy to tell which witch is which.

What goes GNIP-GNOP, GNIP-GNOP?
A Ping-Pong ball bouncing backwards.

How do you slice a Ping-Pong ball?
With a knife.

What do you do to a bad Ping-Pong ball?
Paddle it.

What can you serve, but never eat?
A tennis ball.

Why is tennis such a romantic sport?
Because every game starts with "Love."

Why are fish poor tennis players?
They don't like to get close to the net.

How does a tennis player sneeze?
"A-tennis shoe! A-tennis-shoe!"

Why are waiters good tennis players?
They know how to serve.

Who was the first tennis player in history?
Joseph, in the Bible, because he served in Pharaoh's court.

What is the quietest sport?
Bowling – you can usually hear a pin drop.

Why did all the bowling pins lie down?
They were on strike.

Why do great bowlers play slowly?
Because they have time to spare.

What do bowlers order when they go to a restaurant?
Spare ribs.

Why do they say bowling is good for teenagers?
Because it takes them off the streets and puts them in the alleys.

What did the executioner say to the bowling pins?
"I'll spare you this time."

What can you do with old bowling balls?
Give them to elephants to shoot marbles with.

What present does everyone kick about?
A soccer ball.

Why do soccer players do well in school?
They know how to use their heads.

What has 22 legs and goes CRUNCH
CRUNCH CRUNCH?
A football team eating potato chips.

What do you call a monster that chases a
whole football team?
Hungry!

How do you feel when a football team
lands on you?
Very low.

Why don't skeletons play football?
Because they can't make body contact.

What kitten do you need when a football team tackles you?

A first-aid kit.

Why did the chicken cross the football field?

To score a touchdown.

Why did the silly kid bring a ladder to the ball game?

He wanted to shake hands with the Giants.

Why did giants do push-ups every morning?

To get their extra-size (exercise).

How many feet are there in a football field?

That depends on how many people are standing in it.

When is a football player like a judge?
When he sits on the bench.

What ghost haunts a football team?
The team spirit.

What do you do when a 400-pound football player breaks his big toe?

Call a big toe (tow) truck.

Why couldn't the football player make a phone call?

He couldn't find the receiver.

Why is a football receiver like measles?

Both are catching.

Why did the football coach date the watch?

He wanted to take time out.

Why didn't Cinderella get on the football team?

She had a pumpkin for a coach.

Why was the football coach unpopular?

He was rotten to the end.

What can't a coach ever say to a team of zombies?

"Look alive!"

How do you serve a football player his clam chowder?

In a soup-er bowl.

What happened when the egg got nasty with the football coach?
It was egg-spelled from the game.

What did the coach say when the whole team came down with the flu?
"Win a flu, lose a flu."

What happens when an egg sees a thrilling football game?
It gets egg-cited.

Why was the mayonnaise late for the game?
Because it was dressing.

What would you have to give up if you were the last person in the world?
Team sports.

If a basketball team were chasing a baseball team, what time would it be?

Five after nine.

How did the midget qualify for the basketball team?

He lied about his height.

Why are basketball players tall?

Because their heads are so far from their feet.

How do very tall basketball players greet each other?

They say, "Small world, isn't it?"

What do basketball players order when they go into a restaurant?

Chicken in the Basket.

What do basketball players read in their spare time?

Tall stories.

THAT BASKETBALL PLAYER IS SO TALL—

HOW TALL IS HE?

He's so tall, he has to stand on a ladder to shave himself.

He's so tall, he has to get on his knees just to put his hands in his pockets.

What would you get if you crossed a
basketball with a newborn snake?

A bouncing baby boa.

What is black and white and red all over?
A penguin that has done 100 push-ups.

What do you call a team of Czech basketball players whose games are called off?

Cancelled Czechs (checks).

Why is it hard for basketball players to be neat?

Because they dribble so much.

Why was the termite kicked off the basketball team?

It ate the backboard.

18. GO FOR THE GOLD

Where do judges go to relax?
To the tennis court.

Who keeps locomotives running?
The track coach.

Where do locomotives compete?
At the track meet.

What would you get if you crossed a computer programmer and an Olympic athlete?

A floppy disk-us thrower.

What happened when the discus thrower lost the tournament?

He became discus-ted.

What did the javelin say when it was thrown?

"Oh, spear me! Spear me!"

When does a broad jumper jump highest?

In a leap year.

When can you jump over three men without getting up?

In a checkers game.

Can any broad jumper jump higher than a house?

Yes, a house can't jump.

What kind of house weighs the least?

A lighthouse.

How do you make a lighthouse?
Use balsa wood.

What is brown and white and turns cartwheels?
A brown and white horse pulling a cart.

Why are Boy Scouts so great at gymnastics?
They're always doing good turns.

What season is it when you're on a trampoline?
Springtime.

How do you make fruit punch?
Give it boxing lessons.

Why did the monster give up boxing?
He didn't want to improve his looks.

What has two blades and breathes fire?
  A dragon on ice skates.

What has two wings but doesn't fly?

A hockey team.

What position do monsters play on a hockey team?

Ghoulie.

When a hockey player goes to the barber, does he get a haircut?

No, he gets all of them cut.

What happens when a hockey player tastes a lemon?

He puck-ers up.

What do you need to play ice hockey?

Good ice sight.

What is a ski pro's favorite song?

"There's no business like snow business."

Why did the ski pro say he was an actor?
Because he broke his leg and was in a cast for six months.

What happens when skiers get old?
They go downhill.

Why did the cross-country skier wear only one boot?
He heard the snow was one foot deep.

What winter game do you learn in the fall?
  Ice skating.

What is the hardest thing about learning
to skate?
  The ice.

What time is it when three skiers go ice
skating?
  Wintertime.

When are Olympic swimmers like babies?
  When they do the crawl.

What is the only way a miser will swim?
  Freestyle.

What do you say when you swim into kelp
and it pulls you down?
  "Kelp!"

A lemon and an orange were on a high diving board. The orange jumped, but the lemon didn't. Why?

The lemon was yellow.

What happened when the diver leaped 100 feet into a glass of root beer?

Nothing. It was a soft drink.

Why wouldn't the skeleton jump off the diving board?

It had no guts.

19. BROKEN DOWN ON THE INFORMATION SUPERHIGHWAY

What home computers grow on trees?
Apples.

What is a digital computer?
Someone who counts on his fingers.

What does a proud computer call his little kid?

A microchip off the old block.

What does a computer call its mother and father?

Mama and data.

Where do computers keep their money?

In memory banks.

Why did the silly kid put cheese in her computer?
She wanted to feed the mouse.

What kind of royal cat do you find in a computer?
A Sir Kit (circuit).

What would you get if you crossed a computer and a kangaroo?
I don't know what you would call it, but it would always jump to conclusions.

How do computer scientists sail?
On silicon chips (ships).

What did the scientist get when he crossed the mummy and a stopwatch?
An old-timer.

Why did the scientist like bargains?
Because he was 50% off himself.

What happened when the scientist threw
an elastic band into the computer?
It gave snappy answers.

Why did the farmer put a computer in the hen house?

To make the chickens multiply faster.

What kind of feet do mathematicians have?
  Square feet.

When will a mathematician die?
  When his number is up.

What kind of beat do mathematicians like
to dance to?
  Logarithms.

Why do mosquitoes make great
mathematicians?
  *Because they add to misery, subtract from
  pleasure, divide attention, and multiply
  rapidly.*

Why are bacteria bad mathematicians?
  Because they multiply by dividing.

What figures do the most walking?
  Roman (roamin') numerals.

How is a telephone like arithmetic?
One mistake and you get the wrong number.

How do nuclear scientists relax?
They go fission.

What would you get if you crossed an
elephant and a computer?
A ten-thousand-pound know-it-all.

What would you get if you crossed a
midget and a computer?
A short circuit.

Why did the little computer go to the orthodontist?

To improve its byte.

What did the digital clock say to its mother?

"Look, Ma! No hands!"

The scientist came to his laboratory without a key and found all the windows and doors locked. How did he get in?

He ran round and round the building — until he was all in.

20. MOVING RIGHT ALONG

Why was Adam the best runner of all time?

Because he was first in the human race.

A cabbage, a faucet, and a tomato had a race. How did it go?

The cabbage was ahead (a head), the faucet was running, and the tomato tried to ketchup (catch up).

Why couldn't the orange finish the race?
It ran out of juice.

What race is like the Indianapolis 500 —
but without the apples?
The Indian apple-less 500.

What happened when the race car driver
slammed into a pile of IOUs?
He ran into debt.

What are two auto racers who drive the
same car?
Vroom-mates.

How do fleas start a race?
The starter says, "One, two flea — go!"

How do fireflies start a race?
The starter says, "Ready, set — glow."

How do chickens start a race?
From scratch.

How would a vampire like to see a race finish?

Neck and neck.

Where do you go after you've jogged around a ship ten times?

To the poop deck.

What happens when long distance runners get old?

They go round the bend.

Which big punctuation mark is like a race?

A 40-yard dash.

What do joggers say when they leave you?

"So long – got to run!"

INDEX

Acorns, 162
Acrobats, 55
Actor, 129, 325
Adam, 339
Affection, 121
Airplane, 89, 113
Alligator, 202
Alphabet, 103
Ammonia, 177
Anteaters, 185
Antibiotics, 192
Ants, 95, 101, 291
Apples, 329
Arches, fallen, 213
Arctic Circle, 153
Arithmetic, 335
Art, 31, 133
Artist, 219
Astronauts, 7, 180, 265-267, 269-270, 273
Athlete, 185
Athlete's foot, 198
Atlas, 20
Atmosphere, 109
Atom, 91, 291; bomb, 89, 92
Automobile, 275, 276, 281, 282, 283, 285 (see alsoCar)
Avalanche, 125
Axe, 163
Babies, 257
Bach, 128

Bacteria, 334
Badminton, 130
Bakery, 23
Ball, 65, 66, 71, 136, 296
Banana, 28, 38, 84, 112, 230, 258; boat, 267
Bank robbery, 14, 19, 29
Banks, 25, 34
Barbecue, 23, 99
Barber, 23, 119, 324
Barbershop quartet, 223
Bargains, 332
Barns, 235
Barometer, 80
Bars, 8
Baseball, 59-72, 295-297, 313; players, 247, 297; team, 178
Basketball, 313-316, 318
Bat, 61, 63, 66, 70, 71
Bath, 301
Bathtub, 97, 144
Batman, 259
Batteries, 74
Beach, 106, 255
Bears, 124, 254
Bed, 200, 269
Bedcovers, 203
Bedroll, 256

Bees, 80, 182, 244; hive, 244; keepers, 195
Beef, 46
Bell, 31, 84, 301; church, 33
Bellyaches, 193
Betty Crocker, 65
Bible, 180, 295, 340
Big Dipper, 267
Billy the Kid, 26, 28, 29
Bird, 80, 159; houses, 235
Birthday, 18, 30
Blind man, 178
Blood, 85; pressure, 203; tests, 200
Bloodmobile, 185, 199
Bluebirds, 159
Boat, 120, 121, 185
Boaters, 261
Boomerang, 252
Bowling, 247, 305-306
Boxers, 112, 177, 218, 220-223, 247
Boxing, 322; ring, 219
Boy Scouts, 230, 322
Bread, 11, 95

Breakfast, 101, 150, 299; drink, 77
Breath, 150, 151
Breeze, 174
Bridges, 151, 153
Brontosaurus, 104
Broom, 283
Bucket, 138
Bucks, 233
Buffalo, 49, 250, 251
Bugs Bunny, 243
Building height, 78
Bull, 45, 47, 218
Bumblebee, 80
Burglar, 14
Bus, 224; driver, 171, 215
Bush leagues, 70
Butterfly, 256
Cabbages, 193, 339
Cairo, 185
Cake, 97, 100
Calculator, 82
Calendar, 14
Calves, 41, 43, 45, 49, 95
Campers, 141, 157, 249, 256
Campfire, 232
Camping, 110, 230, 248
Canada Dry, 21
Canary, 80;

344

islands, 105
Candy, 7, 15, 100, 138
Canoe, 157
Capsules, 180
Car, 68, 76, 126, 204, 285, 275, 276, 281, 282, 285, 287, 288, 290
Cards, deck of, 11, 24, 25
Cartwheels, 322
Cash, 34
Cat, 21, 22, 29, 80, 96, 106, 331
Catcher, 178
Catnap, 239
Cats, 276
Catsup, 97
Cattle, 41, 42, 45, 216
Ceiling, 11
Cells, 7
Cement, 87, 129; mixer, 39
Cemetery, 33
Chandelier, 180
Checkers, 141, 321
Checks, 318
Cheerleader, 145, 298-299
Cheetahs, 11, 25
Chef, 68
Chemistry, 89
Chicken, 9, 62, 68, 82, 87, 93, 94, 95, 113, 133,

134, 142, 164, 167, 168, 191, 199, 222, 242, 270-271, 277, 278, 279, 280, 286, 294, 301, 308, 333, 341
Chimneys, 193
Chips, 331
Chiropractor, 185
Chocolate: bars, 8; cake, 25; candy, 138; hot, 31
Choker, 18
Chow, 247
Christmas, 106, 137
Cinderella, 106, 310
Circus, 21
Claustrophobia, 211
Cliff, 131
Clock, 5, 37, 38, 85, 86, 209, 337; grandfather, 168, 221
Clone, 82
Clothes, 66
Clothespins, 11
Clown, 112
Coach, 310-311
Coal, 66; mine, 126
Coat, mink, 280
Coffin, 174
Cold, catching, 171, 174, 176,

177, 194, 206
College, 43
Colt, 35, 231
Combs, 244
Comedian, 112
Comic, 16, 111
Composer, 128
Computer, 21; programmer, 320; scientists, 93, 96, 329-333, 336
Conductor, 82
Confederate soldier, 296
Cook, 12
Cookies, 31
Cookout, 98, 101
Corn, 174; field, 237
Courage, 149
Cow, 33, 42-48, 50, 80, 82, 133, 235, 254, 288
Cowboys, 37, 49, 56, 58, 101, 171, 237, 278
Crabs, 155, 156
Cream, 12; puff, 345
Crime, 228; wave, 108
Criminal, hardened, 39
Croquet, 302
Crossing the Road, 277, 279, 286, 288, 291
Current events,

75
Czechs, 318
Dairy, 132
Dance, 47, 48
Dancers, 193
Dash, 343
Day, rainy, 188
Debt, 341
Deer, 231
Demons, 185
Dentist, 120, 189, 190
Desert, 131, 132
Dessert, favorite, 100
Detective stories, 241
Diamond, 25, 65, 69
Dinosaur, 291
Discus, 213; thrower, 321
Disk, floppy, 320
Diver, 328
Dizzy spells, 195
Doctor, 171, 172, 181, 186, 191, 200, 204, 205, 212, 214, 223
Doctor, 74-75, 169; foot, 198
Dodge City, 27, 29
Dogs, 56, 81, 95, 102, 114, 118, 173, 210, 247, 248, 283, 285
Double-headers, 69, 70

345

Dough, 23
Doughnut, 129
Down, 269
Dracula, Count,
85, 133, 174,
236, 288
Dragon, 67, 323
Dream, 104
Dress, 176, 187
Dressing, 312
Dressmaker, 187
Drink: favorite,
162; soft, 88
Duck, 35, 128,
112, 143, 164,
167, 210, 250,
286
Dumbbell, 301
Eagle, 241
Earache, 170, 174
Earth, 147;
quake, 43, 159
Easter, 135, 138
Eating, 213
Eel, 75
Eggplant, 167
Eggs, 12, 88, 117,
135, 138, 164,
167, 168, 312
Elastic band, 332
Electricity, 75, 82
Elephant, 17, 78,
108, 170, 181,
189, 192, 256,
279, 284, 291,
299
306, 336; sand-
wich, 95
Elevator, 177

Elk, 180
Entertainment, 47
Errors, 63
Eve, 91
Executioner, 17,
137, 305
Exercise, 185,
206; light, 180
Exterminator, 6
Eye: chart, 188;
doctor, 187
Eyes, 63, 230;
sore, 187
Facsimilies, 171
Families, sick,
171
Fan mail, 159
Fans, 65, 66
Farm, 236, 238
Farmer, 44, 167,
180, 228, 235,
237, 243, 244,
254, 277, 333
Farmhouse, 236
Faucet, 339
Feathers, 87
Feet, 121, 122,
124
Fencer, 182, 225,
226
Fire, 13, 110, 220;
engine, 283; for-
est, 141, 159
Firecracker, 139
Fireflies, 138,
243, 341
Fish, 105, 107,
126, 151, 183,
254, 303

Fisherman, 14
Fishing, 259
Fission, 335
Flat tire, 284, 290
Fleas, 56, 118,
178, 341
Fleecing, 246
Flies, 59, 61, 65,
70, 71, 101, 243
Flights, 8
Florida Keys, 151
Flu, 35, 193, 201,
312
Flying saucers,
267, 274 see
also UFOs
Fodder, 288
Food, 93-102, 143
Foot, 220
Football, 145;
player, 143, 146,
243, 307-312;
team, 144, 238,
309;
tryouts, 254
Fourth of July,
139
Fowl, 68
Frankenstein
monster, 133,
295
French fries, 100
Frog, 88, 100,
102, 122, 135,
161, 239, 256,
283, 294
Gag, 16
Galaxies, 273,
274

Game, 107, 136,
179, 312
Gangster, 16
Gardeners, 237
Gas, 281; tank,
287
Geese, 163
Geologist, 100,
140, 141, 149,
150
Germ, 206
Ghost, 309;
towns, 21
Ghouls, 102
Giants, 308
Giraffe, 170, 171
Glove, 178
Glue, 37
Goat, 28, 232,
243
Goose, 286
Gorilla, 76
Grandfather
clock, 221
Grapes, 23, 268
Grass, 193, 235
Gravity, 87
Great Lakes, 151
Gum, 93, 95
Gun, 35, 36, 37;
fastest, 22
Guts, 328
Gymnastics, 322
Hair, 241; dryer,
234
Haircut, 245, 324
Hamburgers, 96,
97
Hamlet, 247

Hand, 220
Handedness, 31
Hands, shaking, 218
Hang gliding, 17
Hangmen, 17, 18
Hanky, 174
Hare, 243
Hat, 37, 39
Hay, 58; fever, 193
Headaches, 193
Health club, 134
Health food store, 182
Heart, broken, 172
Heights, fear of, 269
Helium, 186
Helmet, 145
Hen, 163, 168, 222; house, 333
Hide and seek, 133, 179
Hiker, 113, 121, 123, 125, 141, 143
Hill, 178
Hitchhiker, 284
Hives, 195
Hockey, 324; player, 129
Hog, 180
Holdups, 19, 20, 23
Hole, 29
Holiday, 103
Hollywood, 226

Home, 49, 72; run, 70
Homework, 273
Hondas, 285
Honey, 244
Honor roll, 99
Hootenanny, 243
Horse, 35, 49, 51, 53-55, 57-58, 230, 235, 278, 322; wild, 233
Hospital, 196-197, 199, 201, 202, 206-208, 231; bed, 201; dog, 200
Hot dog, 99
House, 321
Humpty Dumpty, 149
Hurricane names, 157
Hydrogen bomb, 92
Ice cream, 299; cone, 35
Ice hockey, 325
Ice skating, 323, 327
Indianapolis 500, 341
Indigestion, 180
Infections, 185, 192
Inning, 295
Insects, 197, 243
Instinct, 216
Instruments, musical, 126

Invention, 88
Invisible Man, 80
Jail, 5-18
Jailer, 7
James, Jesse, 21, 22, 33, 35
Javelin, 321
Jeans, 56
Jekyll, Dr., 255, 288
Jeweler, 7
Jogging, 343
Joker, 11
Jokes, 112, 249
Judge, 308, 319
Judo, 218
Jumper, broad, 321
Jungle, 11
Kangaroos, 196, 331
Karate, 216-219
Kelp, 327
Kentucky Fried Chicken, 138
Kermit, 135
Killer, 6
King Kong, 116, 119
Kitchen, 143
Kitten, 308
Kung fu, 177
Laboratory, 338
Lake, 121, 122, 126, 151
Lamb, 228
Language, fowl, 9
Laryngitis, 177
Lassie, 109

Lawyers, 250
Lead, 87
Leap year, 321
Lee, Bruce, 177, 217
Lemon, 31, 84, 324, 328
Letters, 141, 159
Lettuce, 228
Librarians, 197
License plate, 283
Lighthouse, 321, 322
Lightning, 82, 146
Line, 254; firing, 227
Lion, 60, 97, 289
Litterbug, 228
Little Red Riding Hood, 33
Loafers, 8
Lobster, 63
Loch Ness monster, 300
Locomotives, 319
Logarithms, 334
Lone Ranger, 324
Looks, 322
Lullaby, 141
Magnet, 158, 230
Mall, 288
Maps, 117, 290
Marbles, 179
Mars, 263-265
Marshall Dill, 27
Martian, 77, 263-265, 270, 272, 273

347

Masks, 173
Matador, 218
Matches, 110, 220
Math book, 191
Mathematicians, 334
Mayonnaise, 312
McDonald, Ronald, 213
Measles, 178, 179, 310
Meat: ball, 47; loaf, 46
Medicine, 172, 180; cabinet, 198
Memories, bad, 281
Mice, 117, 119
Mickey Mantle, 65
Mickey Mouse, 195
Microchip, 330
Microscope, 206
Midget, 313, 336
Milk, 31, 132; shakes, 43
Miner, 126
Miser, 327
Mistakes, 173
Mistletoe, 269
Moaning, 182
Money, 44, 291, 330
Monkey, 60, 77; wrench, 76
Monster, 307,

322, 324
Moon, 46, 109, 147, 148, 265, 269
Moose, 233
Moses, 180
Mosquitoes, 158, 226, 334
Mother, 235
Moths, 228, 257
Motorcycle, 112, 114-115; riders, 195
Mount Everest, 131
Mountain: climbers, 131; top, 229
Mountaineers, 229
Mouse, 109, 114, 331
Movie director, 97
Muffins, 143
Mummies, 64, 107, 203, 331
Mushroom, 249
Music, 48, 97, 200
Musical instruments, 126
Musicians, 96, 126
Mustache, 50
Nail, 220, 284
Nature, 147-162
Nightmares, 53
Noise, 248, 269

North Pole, 61, 114, 152
Nuclear scientist, 91, 92
Nurse, 187, 203
Nutcracker, 240
Nuts, 27, 75, 240
Ocean, 153, 154, 155, 157, 225, 262
Octopuses, 110
Oil, 87, 171
Ointment, 180
Old MacDonald, 188
Old West, 19, 21, 53
Old-timer, 331
Olympic athlete, 213, 320
Olympics, 129
One-handed man, 279
Opener, 68
Opera, 259
Operating room, 183
Operations, 171, 172, 173
Opticians, 187
Optometrists, 187
Orange, 328, 340
Orchestra, 82, 128
Orthodontist, 190, 337
Otter, 194, 286
Outlaws, 19-40, 69

Owl, 77, 165, 166, 205, 241-243
Pain, 188, 202
Painter, 31
Pancakes, 101, 206
Pants, 11
Paper, 174
Paratrooper, 78-79
Parrots, 78-80, 139, 196
Parties, 8, 75, 93
Patience, 104
Patients, 204
Pea, 218
Penguin, 105, 317
Perfume, 253
Personality, dual, 182
Phantoms, 106
Photocopier, 171
Photographer, 14
Piano, 10, 72
Pickles, 23, 25, 27, 99, 162
Picnic, 101, 102
Pictures, 8, 31
Pigs, 59, 109, 135, 136, 198, 219
Pill, 178; sleeping, 198
Pilots, 117; airline, 8
Pinch hitter, 63-64
Ping-Pong, 133, 303

Pirate, 237

Pistol, 35

Pizza, 93, 119

Planet of the Apes, 267

Plasma, 185

Play, camp, 113

Plumber, 172

Pneumonia, 177

Pocket, 82

Poison ivy, 141

Poker, 24, 25

Pole, 239

Police, 8, 292, 301

Ponchos, 49

Ponies, 197

Pony Express, 53

Pop, cold, 114

Porcupine, 52, 85, 123

Portugal, 163

Posse, 22

Potato: field, 238; sweet, 126, 238

Potatoes, 223

Practice, 172

Prince, 130

Prisoners, 7, 8, 10, 15, 17

Problems, 191

Promises, 172

Prune, 282

Psychiatrist, 43, 74, 181, 182

Punch, 322

Punctuality, 85

Pup, 159; tents, 248

Pupils, 187

Push-ups, 317

Queen, 66

Rabbit, 111, 112, 119, 194, 225, 239, 285, 287, 288; hole, 234; hutch, 243

Race, 99, 237, 261, 340-343; car, 35, 106, 126; horse, 342; human, 339

Race car driver, 341

Racket, tennis, 129, 131

Racquets, 11

Radio, 129

Rain, 169, 188, 231

Raindrop, 151

Ranchers, 237

Rat, 190

Referees, 145

Reindeer, 138

Resort hotel, 239

Restaurant, 32, 41, 97, 305, 313

Rheumatism, 195

Rifle, 36

River, 25, 121, 153, 262

Road, 275, 291

Roast beef, 82

Robbery, 40

Robin, 66, 259; Hood, 6

Robot, 73, 75, 76, 90, 122

Rock: concerts, 140; star, 126-127

Rocket, 269

Rodeo, 56

Rods, 14, 35, 282

Rolling Stones, 125

Roman numerals, 334

Romans, 117

Rooster, 86

Rope, 235

Rubber band factory, 14

Runners, 319, 339, 343

Running, 250, 281

Russians, 117

Safari, 125

Safecrackers, 29

Sailors, 25, 178

Saloons, 56

Saltine, 29

San Andreas fault, 149

Sandpaper, 65

Santa Claus, 211

Saturn, 269

Scarecrows, 133

School, 70; medical, 210, 212

Science, 73-92

Scientist, 274; nuclear, 335

Score, 295

Scuba diver, 260

Sea horse, 261

Seashore, 292

Sentence, 8

Setter, 247

Shake, strawberry, 21

Shark, 77, 261

Sheep, 17, 56, 84, 138, 245, 246, 254

Sheet, 203

Shellfish, 301

Sheriff, 9, 12, 21, 23

Ships, 7, 157

Shock absorbers, 75

Shoe, 53, 114, 122; store, 8

Shortstop, 68

Show, 17, all-star, 55; talent, 166

Shower, 7, 184m 267

Shrub, 143

Sickness, 177

Silver, 324

Singers, 124

Six-shooter, 227

Skateboard, 289

Skating, ice, 327

Skeleton, 105, 307, 328

Ski pro, 325

Skiers, 326

Skillet, 78

Skunk, 77, 216, 223, 252-254

Sky diving, 259

349

Sleep, 113, 238, 252, 270

Sleeping pills, 198

Sleeping bag, 249, 252, 256

Sleighing, 137

Slippers, 84

Smelling, 254

Snack, 93; favorite, 92, 246

Snake, 249, 256, 275, 316

Sneaker, 8, 299, 300

Sneeze, 174, 175, 203, 303

Snow, 326

Snowstorm, 43

Soap, 17

Soccer, 307

Socks, 25, 53

Soda pop, 68

Songbirds, 105

Song, favorite, 99, 198, 244, 325

South Pole, 152

Space, outer, 7, 148

Spaceships, 262

Spectacle, 88

Speech, 45

Spider, 59, 96, 231

Spit, 50

Sponge, 75

Springtime, 322

Spy, 153

Squid, 210

Squirrel, 240, 241

Stars, shooting, 266

Statue of Liberty, 175

Steeple, church, 33

Steers, 45, 276

Stick up, 37

Stole, 30

Stomach, 213; empty, 97, 327

Stone, 77, 126, 129, 141, 149

Stopwatch, 331

Story, short, 281

Stove, 249

Stream, 121

Strikes, 65, 66

String, 147

Sugar bowl, 243

Summer, 103, 105, 106, 114, 122, 149; camp, 131

Sun, 147, 265

Surfboard, 261

Surfer, 27

Surgeons, 74, 112, 172, 173, 214; plastic, 184

Swallowing, 176

Sweet potato, 126

Sweets, 7, 15, 31, 100

Swimming, 106, 107, 241, 257, 261, 327, 328; pool, 108, 259

Swordfish, 225

Tablets, 180

Tackle, 254

Tail light, 281

Talk, 37, 99, 177

Talkers, slowest, 8

Tapeworms, 195

Tea, 267

Teachers, 63, 187

Team spirit, 309

Team sports, 312

Teenagers, 305

Teeth, 37; buck, 190

Telephone, 335; operator, 61

Tellers, 14

Temperature, 78, 87, 159

Tennis, 129-131, 303, 304, 319; court, 168; players, 11

Tents, 248, 249

Tepee, 110

Termite, 318

Texas, 82

Thermometer, 77, 78

Thieves, 14, 17, 108

Throat, sore, 170, 171, 178

Tick, 228

Time, 5, 38

Timepiece, 168

Tire, 109, 284

Tissue, 174

Toad, 133, 161, 239, 274, 282, 283; see also Frog

Tomatoes, 49, 339

Tombstone, 90

Toothache, 188

Tooth, sore, 19

Towns, ghost, 21

Track meet, 319

Tractor, 235

Trains, 19

Trampoline, 322

Transylvania, 117

Trapeze flyer, 293

Travel, 117, 120, 121; agent, 215

Trees, 162, 185, 301, 329

Trek, 131, 132

Turkey, 208, 279

Turtles, 65, 286

Tuscaloosa, Alabama, 190

TV set, 142

Twig, 162

Two-timers, 11

Typewriter, 85

UFO, 78

Umbrella, 243

Umpire, 61-63, 66

Underwear, thermal, 324

Unions, 66

Vacation, 104-105, 109-110,

350

118, 246
Valentine's Day, 136
Vampires, 70. 130, 199, 200, 342
Vegetables, 121, 228, 238
Veterinarian, 169
Video cassettes, 195
Virus, 171
Vitamin, 182
Voice, 171
Volcano, 158
Volkswagens, 281

Waiters, 94, 97, 304
Waitress, 274
Walking, 281
Walls, 11
Watches, 7, 11, 63, 223, 310
Water, 88, 151, 184; fall, 153
Wave, tidal, 258
Weather, 167, 231
Weeds, 263
Week, 187
Weightlifter, 147, 301

Werewolves, 137
West, 21, 23; 28; old, 19, 53
West, wild, 250
Whistle, 37
Whistler's mother, 206
Wind, 150; strong, 174
Winter day, 220
Witch doctor, 185
Witches, 98, 119, 249, 302
Wolves, 120
Woodpecker, 241
Worm, 237, 259

Wrestler, 146, 182, 224, 225
X-rays, 198
Yacht, 190
Yankees, 296
Yellowstone National Park, 124
Zebra, 106
Zeppelin, 186
Zombies, 109, 311
Zoo, 60